All About Arctic Hares

Kerrily Sapet

EZ READERS
AN IMPRINT OF MITCHELL LANE PUBLISHERS

CREATING YOUNG NONFICTION READERS

EZ Readers offer nonfiction for beginning readers in PreK through first grade, using simple language, clear illustrations, and engaging facts to build vocabulary and confidence.

TIPS FOR READING NONFICTION WITH BEGINNING READERS

Talk about Nonfiction

Begin by explaining that nonfiction books give us information that is true. The book will be organized around a specific topic or idea, and we may learn new facts through reading.

Look at the Parts

Most nonfiction books have helpful features. Our *EZ Readers* include color photographs and graphic aids, a table of contents, a glossary, and an index. Share the purpose of these features with your reader.

Color Photos and Graphic Aids

A lot of information can be found by "reading" photos, charts, maps, and other graphic aids found within nonfiction texts. Help your reader learn more about the different ways information can be displayed.

Table of Contents

Located at the front of the book, this list shows the big ideas within the text and the page numbers where they can be found.

Glossary

Located at the back of the book, the glossary defines key words and phrases that are related to the topic. These words and phrases can be found in the text in colored type.

Index

Located at the back of the book, an index is an alphabetical list of topics and the page numbers where they can be found.

With a little help and guidance about reading nonfiction, you can feel good about introducing a young reader to the world of *EZ Readers* nonfiction books.

EZ Readers is an imprint of:

Mitchell Lane
PUBLISHERS

2001 SW 31st Avenue
Hallandale, FL 33009
mitchelllanepub.com

First Edition, 2026.

Author: Kerrily Sapet
Editor: Morgan Brody

ISBN 979-8-89260-849-7 (library binding)
ISBN979-8-90145-042-0 (paperback)
ISBN 979-8-89260-946-3 (ebook)

LC record available at https://lccn.loc.gov/2025950871

Photo credits: Photo credits: Adobe, Pixasquare, cover, 1, 2, 3, 4, 8, 12, 15, 16,18, 21, 22, 23, 24; Adobe, Tukinoto, cover, 1; Shutterstock, Nick Dale Photo, cover, 1; Adobe, NikolaM, 3, 9, 10, 14, 19; Shutterstock, Pressmaster, 5; Shutterstock, Paul Loewen, 6–7; Shutterstock, Paul Loewen, 9; Shutterstock, evgenii mitroshin, 10–11, 22; Alamy, Matthias Breiter, 13, 22; Shutterstock, Sophia Granchinho, 14; Shutterstock, Jukka Jantunen, 19, 22; Shutterstock, Sophia Granchinho, 20; Shutterstock, Andrei Stepanov, 21; Shutterstock, grayjay, 22; Wikimedia Commons, iNaturalist, 22; Shutterstock, uznetsova Julia, 22; Shutterstock, Fotogro, 22

Table of Contents

White Winter Surprise. 4
Hare Watching. 8
Looking for Food 15
Where Do Arctic Hares Live? 17
Arctic Hares Families and the Future. . .18
Parts of an Arctic Hare 21
Glossary 22
Quiz. 23
Further Reading. 24
On the Internet 24
Index. 24
About the Author. 24

White Winter Surprise

Imagine you've stepped into a snowy land. Wind swirls around you. Your coat protects you from the cold.

Something jumps across the snow. It looks like a rabbit, but it's the size of a small dog. An **arctic** hare! Its fur is white like the snow. Arctic hares live on the **tundra**—a place so cold that the ground is frozen.

Hare Watching

The hare has thick, warm fur. You can see its short tail and dark eyes. Its black eyelashes shade its eyes from the white snow—like wearing sunglasses.

HOPPING HARES!

Arctic hares can hop on their back legs like kangaroos. They can also jump over people.

HOPPING HARES!

Arctic hares look like snowballs when they curl up tight.

The hare disappears. It's gone into a **burrow**—a tunnel in the snow. Hares snuggle inside burrows to stay warm.

You don't hear any noises in the burrow. Arctic hares are quiet. They **communicate** by moving their ears, scratching or licking. Sometimes they stand up and box each other.

HOPPING HARES!

Arctic hares eat snow when they are thirsty.

Looking for Food

You see the hare again. Its nose twitches. It smells a plant under the snow. The hare digs with its strong claws. It pulls the plant out of the ground with its teeth. Arctic hares eat plants, roots, and **moss**.

It's almost nighttime. You see more hares. Arctic hares are **nocturnal**. They sleep during the day and are awake at night. They live in groups called warrens.

Where Do Arctic Hares Live?

Arctic Hare Families and the Future

Baby hares are called **leverets**. Leverets stay in their burrows. They are about the size of a banana. Leverets can hop within minutes of being born.

HOPPING HARES!

A mother gives birth to about six leverets at one time.

Arctic hares can live three to five years. They need the snow and ice on Earth to survive. Someday you might see a real arctic hare.

Parts of an Arctic Hare

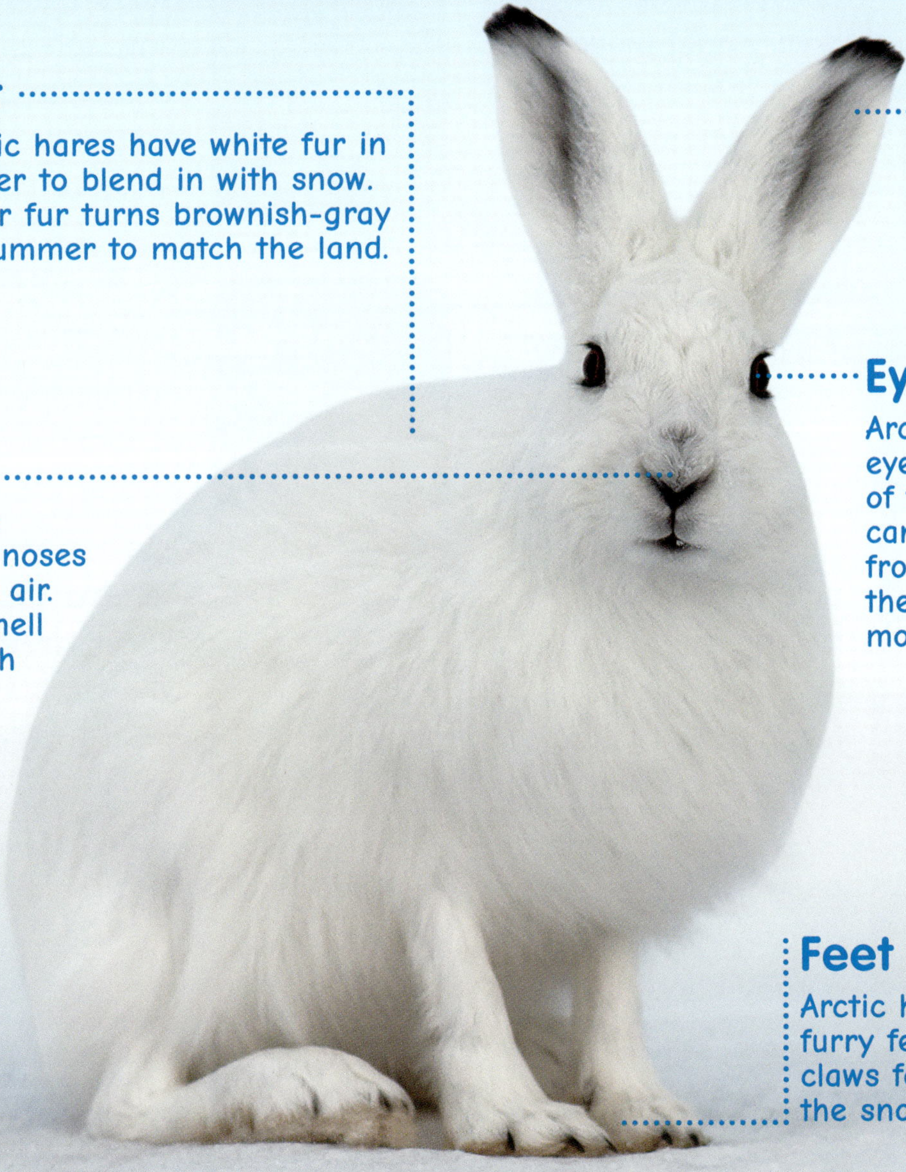

Fur

Arctic hares have white fur in winter to blend in with snow. Their fur turns brownish-gray in summer to match the land.

Ears

Arctic hares have long ears. They turn their ears to find the source of a sound.

Eyes

Arctic hares have eyes on the sides of their heads. They can see what's in front and behind them without moving their heads.

Nose

Arctic hares twitch their noses to smell the air. They can smell food beneath the snow.

Feet

Arctic hares have furry feet with long claws for digging in the snow and ice.

Glossary

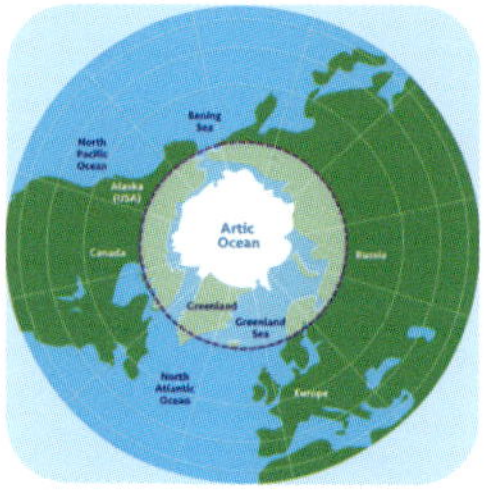

arctic (ARK-tik) a very cold place near the top of the Earth where there is lots of ice and snow

burrow (BUHR-oh) a safe place where an animal lives or rests

communicate (kuh-myoon-i-kayt) to share ideas or feelings by making noise or moving

leveret (LEV-er-ett) a baby hare

moss (MAW-s) a tiny, soft plant that looks like a green carpet growing on rocks or the ground

nocturnal (NOCK-ter-nul) an animal that is awake at night and sleeps during the day

tundra (TUN-dra) a cold, treeless land where the ground stays frozen

Quiz

1. Do arctic hares live in the woods?

   A. Yes   B. No

2. Do arctic hares have warm fur?

   A. Yes   B. No

3. Do arctic hares eat birds?

   A. Yes   B. No

4. Are arctic hare babies called leverets?

   A. Yes   B. No

ANSWER KEY
DO NOT PEEK!

ANSWER KEY:

1. No
2. Yes
3. No
4. Yes

Further Reading

Emminizer, Theresa. *Hopping Arctic Hares.* New York, NY: Rosen Publishing, 2021.

Geron, Erin. *Desert Hare or Arctic Hare (Wild World: Hot and Cold Animals).* New York, NY: Scholastic, 2022.

Maloney, Brenna. *Arctic (Wild World: Habitats Day and Night).* New York, NY: Scholastic, 2024.

On the Internet

Arctic Hares

https://www.gettyimages.com/search/2/film?family=creative&phrase=arctic%20hare

Watch videos of arctic hares eating, hopping and digging in the snow.

Arctic Hares

https://nhpbs.org/natureworks/arctichare.htm

Read more and see pictures of arctic hares.

A Walk in the Arctic

https://mybigworld.scholastic.com/issues/2020-21/010121.html

Learn about the snowy world where arctic hares live.

Index

babies, 18–19, 22
burrow, 10–11, 18–19, 22
families, 18–19, 22
food, 14–15
fur, 7, 8, 21
nocturnal, 16, 22
size, 7, 18
sounds, 12
tundra, 7, 22

About the Author

Kerrily Sapet has written more than 40 books for kids. She lives near Chicago with her family. She had a pet rabbit named Grover when she was growing up. It was brown and much smaller than an arctic hare. Sapet has never seen an arctic hare. She hopes to see one someday.